©Rebecca Puterbaugh
ISBN: 978-1-79486-538-9

shadows form light

Rebecca Puterbaugh

For Ruby -- my twin flame and lifelong best friend.
May the arms of the Mother cradle you in peace and love.
I will see you in another lifetime.
Thank you.

~

For my daughter -- this love for you has
been light guiding me through shadows.
Your ocean eyes and boundless spirit have been lanterns.
Thank you.

~

For my friends who have seen my grief
and patiently refused to look away.
You know who you are.
Thank you.

Trigger Warning

Some of the poems within this book contain references to suicide and suicide ideation.

If you struggle with depression, anxiety, and/or suicidal thoughts, please reach out to someone you trust, and get both professional and personal help.

You have a reason to be here.
Let others help you bear the weight of your grief,
so you can find your Reason for Being.

The phone number for the National Suicide Prevention Lifeline in the United States is
1-800-273-8255
and is available 24 hours a day. They also have an online chat for those uncomfortable with picking up the phone.

Take care of yourself.
I hope to meet you one day.

"Every man casts a shadow; not his body only, but his imperfectly mingled spirit. This is his grief. Let him turn which way he will, it falls opposite to the sun; short at noon, long at eve. Did you ever see it?"

(Thoreau)

~

"Grief can be the garden of compassion.
If you keep your heart open through everything,
your pain can become your greatest ally
in your life's search for love and wisdom."

(Rumi)

Integration Spell, November 2019

Fear! Ego-born
monster that whispers
inadequacy and scarcity
at the threshold
between Who I've Been
and Who I Will Be:

I'm not scared of you.
I am far more powerful.

You think you seize me,
but it is I who seize you,
and devour your shadowy bones,
cold blood dripping down my
grinning and grimacing chin.

Banishment has never worked
on your persistent and varied form.

So instead I consume you,
digest your pain and suffering
in my gut's odd life-death womb;
take only your wisdom,
and cast away the rest.

I am the Devourer,
Great Digester of Shadows.

They are my clay
with which to form light.
I step over the threshold
Whole and Holy,
my light my guide,

my pain
my advisor.

December, 2018

<u>4 am,</u>

and poems burst
from my fingers
as though grief
broke a dam
in my spirit,
and I must cry
with words,
just words,
a quiet song
lacking rhythm
but dripping
with holy.

<u>It's back again</u>

the quiet longing
to fade into the wind
and become the green growing things
crawling up the summits and buttes.

The days stretch before me,
and I
want to forget time --

become the crow's call
and the hawk's wing.

I want to let my skin
break apart, thread by
luminous thread,
and lose my mind,
find divinity.

Humanity is
too heavy a burden today.

I am choking on it.

Free me from reality.

Take me to where the land
has a heartbeat like a drum
and a song like a scream like a
feather on the wind.

The first morning

of the new year
and everything is covered
in the first true frost
of the season.

But I have lived in winter
for weeks now.

Right when I've let myself forget,

it hits me out of nowhere
in the middle of the produce aisle
where a red flesh dragonfruit
sits, innocent and lacking fragrance,
a consequence of distance traveled.

Her face splashes across my eyes:
tropical laughter,
rounding belly,
horseback beneath palm trees;
letters in the mail, all these years . . .
the vision of a
swollen, purple, choking face.

& it sickens me
that you'll never taste
the fruit of this life again.

I am a cliche,
crying and dazed in the produce aisle.

I buy it anyway.

I'd rather taste your presence,

memories on my tongue,
than pretend to not need
the ghost of your voice on my lips.

I wanted to live

vividly, yet sustainably
like a campfire
on the river's shore
with the late evening sun
illuminating insects and moss
in gold
as one breathes
the living, wild air.

But your suicide
weighed on me,
dropping a veil
between my heart
and beauty.

I am scared,
a little,
of joy, now.

It is so easily
a loss of control.

Surrender
is so easily

insanity.

I used to chase it
(spontaneity, an embodied
form of surrender)
Like some people
chase storms --
I craved it
with a desperate
hunger.

Now the craving
is edged with fear,
like thunder at the edge
of the luminous dusk,

ominous,

though I know
it's only tearing away
the past.

Millennials and Gen Zers, 2019

Depression
Anxiety
Suicide

Skyrocketing
rates,
symptoms
of
a
deeper
collective
animal
despair,

a
silent
howling
for
an
awakening
we're
terrified
may
not

arrive

in
time.

<u>I craved</u>

to be filled

Yet nothing
fills enough.

"Being stressed

is not the same as
wanting to die"

I whisper to myself
as a great weight
crushes my chest

begging

to be released.

Scream

Has anyone noticed
there is nowhere to scream in this city?
I know, I know --
as a rule, people are generally scared of screaming.
And I hate it. It is a spear of pain in my chest.
There's nowhere to stand and howl,
nowhere to rip my chest open and let the blood flow into the
street and make the trees grow again . . .
there's nowhere to explode
into a million pieces of flesh and bone and stone and light
and

shadows.

There are plenty of shadows, technically speaking:
rectangular
shadows crawling blue-grey across the pavement
while I search for sunset,
climbing concrete to chase golden rays
back to where I swear to goddess I came from --
the North, the West,
where mountains melt glacial waters into sea.

But . . . I want uneven shadows.

I desperately crave them.
I want shadows of peaks that rise, sharp silhouettes
against the bloody hallelujah crust of dawn.
I want shadows of waves that are obliterated and created
every minute.

I want *my* shadow, dancing,
and I'm no longer in my head that won't stop screaming
silently
because the screaming has been consumed by the trees
and the cold clear air
and all that is left is

this body.

This scarred body,
this sensuous body
that I love and hate so much
because it can dance
and it can sing
and it keeps me, sometimes forcibly, here,

and all too often I am scared to let it dance
and sing
because here in these city streets
its singing feels like screaming.

It wants to scream.

And it wants
you to scream.

It wants to fall on its knees
on the highest building
as the sun dies
maybe for the last time
and begin a symphony
of everybody
stopping
and collapsing
and letting go
of the animalistic
existential
cry
bursting
at the seams.

But there's nowhere.
There's nowhere to scream.

And I'm bursting
at these badly sewn seams.

You do not know

how terribly tired I am.
You don't know because
I've never told you,
and you've never asked,
and the more I want you to know
the less capable I feel
of telling you unsolicited.

I tell you, "I'm tired,"
and we find ourselves talking
about what time we woke up,
the sounds outside last night,
our dreams, the moon,
what planet is in retrograde.

I am scared to tell you
what sort of tired I am --
the tired that has little to do
with the hours of consciousness
and everything to do
with the steady, ever-present thrum
of the beast sitting on my chest.

I am scared to tell you,

and you've never asked.

The rain sang to us.

I fell asleep to it
        and music
        and the soft breathing
                of another man
                (my escape
                for one night.)
I feel less and less
        that I am capable.
Yet I know that I am.
        Yet I know that I am not.

Alice Walker writes
that we must turn madness
into flowers.

I feel less and less stable
with every day that goes by.

Please --

Someone,
plant me.

Show me how flowers can grow

from this anguish.

Twin Flame

I walk with the ghost
of her noose
encircling my neck.

A shadow jewelry
no one sees
but I always feel.

The crackle
of her fire,
galloping hooves

following me,
a shadow
within my own.

I walk,
and she walks -

the living,
and the beloved dead.

Constellations

why are the stars clearer
in the middle of the crossroads

where my longing
and eternity mingle,
like lovers

between the have-been
and the perhaps,

the should-haves
and the will

The Hawk and the Ant

The soaring highs,
riding on the wings of a red-tailed hawk,
climbing with the clouds
through the kaleidoscopic blue,
only coming down to ground
and rest before the next
soulful flight . . .

Now the trenchuous lows,
crawling like an ant
along the kitchen counter,
knowing honey is seeping somewhere,
longing for the liquid amber fragrance
(honey, honeyed heart,
spirit drips with it,
steeping sweet light,
warm and buzzing with life).

There is a pressure in my chest,
this time:
an opening, maybe;
or rather,
the moment before the fabric breaks,
when the fibers are stretching, slowly

tearing: I don't know.

And I can't sugarcoat my way to meaning this time.
Words don't come easily this time,
dripping my story with the richness and sublimity of Story.
Vulnerability, I've discovered,
loses its power when shared casually.

I don't want to tear myself open
for whoever wants to know.
My pain is a tribute,
a prayer, a blessing:

the only tears I want to shed
are the ones in the sacred wheel
of flesh and bone and stones
and trees (always, the trees).

It's there, after all,
that I remember again the truth:
I am both the hawk
and the ant.

<u>I'm realizing that my problem may not,</u>

in fact, be an inability to love stillness,
or a difficulty in being who I imagine
I once, perhaps, was.

In fact, it may not be a problem at all,
only a forgetfulness that weighs
on the senses and dulls the taste
of the life that licks my lips.

Who I once was does not exist,
and in fact I question whether that I
existed at all, because now
I am, quite simply, tired,

and rather lonely, but I'm lonely when
I'm being loved as well, so I know
that I'm tired not because of too
much activity, nor am I without company --

no, I believe now that I'm tired
only of complexity, the manufactured kind
that doesn't realize that nature
is a series of patterns, fractals, repeated

in ever more intricate and beautiful ways;
and I'm lonely because these walls
are suffocating and I want more company
than people with screens acting as a

third-party, facilitating a connection
that, without pixels and data, could
root deeper. I want to mingle with your roots
the way trees do -- beneath dark soil,

where, unadvertised, no hashtags, we embrace
and whisper secrets, exchange ecstasies
down where light is the electricity
between my fingers and yours,

where we drew it down from branches
full of activity, and now we're
grounding each other, feeding each other,
forming a vast network invisible

only to those who look no further
than a mutual reaction to
the illusions projected by flickering blues.

We could be so much more,

and I am tired.

Come root deeper with me.

<u>I am a slut</u>

of the soul

I'll open to strangers

but fear my friends

Take me to

where the rain
kisses the ocean
back

Take me to
where the rain
feeds the forest
sky

Take me to
where the rain
makes love to
my lips

so I can remember
what eternity
feels like.

I'm waiting
Inspired by the writings of Charles deLint

I'm waiting for who I was
to catch up to who I'll be,
and waiting for miracles
to arise from the liminal streets.

I'm waiting for miracles
to arise from the liminal streets,
and waiting for remembrance
to illuminate the spirit within me.

I'm waiting for remembrance
to illuminate the spirit within me,
and waiting for absurd good news
to remind how magical the world can be.

I'm waiting for absurd good news
to remind how magical the world can be,
and waiting for who I was
to catch up to who I'll be.

I'm waiting for miracles
to arise from the liminal streets,
and beginning again to think

that the creation of miracles
is actually up to me.

Anger roils in my throat,

but the volcano already blew;
magma runs down my skin,
and it should burn, this skin should melt
but I feel powerful,
all lipstick and curves,
Pele in my bones
                again.

Maybe it's just that I've
felt desperate and almost numb for months now;
it could be that I've been fighting
against the seductive call of destruction,
and fury feels so good, feels Alive;
this must be what fireweed feels like,
rising rising
                from the ash.

Yet, I know the magma will slow,
its crawl will halt and harden;
what then? How long will it take
for sweet rains to grow a jungle
upon blackened flesh?

I don't know, I've never known.

For now, maybe I'll just
dance
with the fire.

Labyrinth

There are no side tracks
just one path
twisting
dancing
turning
even when I feel lost
I am moving
ever forward
deeper
into my soul
then turning
and dancing
back into life.

transformation spell

a green
spiraling
snake
lived
on
my
chest
all
night;

when
I
awoke,
nothing
was
the
same.

I
had
Remembered
myself
again.

Intention

give me more
candle flame curling tea steam
on rainy evenings

more depth
breathing liminal light shadows
where the dawn beckons

more vibrancy
green growing dying colorful things
in the sweet daylight

more spirit
laughing crying dancing incense moon
at sacred midnight

give me more

more
        pause

more
        center

more
        creation

more
more
more
        lush

in the
chaos
of
this one spiraling
fractal
beautiful terrible
life.

(inspired by First, We Make The Beast Beautiful *by Sarah Wilson)*

Sehnsucht (noun)

An intense yearning
for something far-off
and indefinable.

--

Divine Discontent
Endless Questioning
That Spurs Creation

If I cannot always be at peace,
help me to love this
Sacred Anxious Chaos
that roils ever on in my chest.

Turn this feeling of
not-right-ness
into a meaning, a mission
that quickens the Spirit.

If I must be, in the end, alone

in suffering,
let it be a hallowed place.

Steep me in paradox:
a strange ecstasy
in the midst of pain,
like I am in labor,
birthing life,
turning screams

into creation.

Love me

when I push you away

and my amygdala calms.
The bubble of fear bursts,

the sun warm on my face
like it's the first day of spring

and when the hawk calls,
my Spirit lifts

again.

<u>My friend said,</u>

well-meaning,
from outside
the gilded facade
of my walls,
that people find me
fascinating

and that hurt more
than all the resentments
and insults I've ever
endured.

Please don't find me
fascinating.

Find me
human
and knock,
quietly but
persistently,
on my door.

You came to me in my dreams

beside a rushing summer river
near a bridge glimmering in warm light.
Your arms encircled me,
and I clutched you, crying in joy.

"Would you believe me
if I told you
I wasn't really here?"
you said in a tone of
compassion, forgiveness, love.

"No, I wouldn't,"
I replied, laughing, unbelieving.

And just like that,
my arms were empty.

I turned,
and beheld your husband's face.

"She was here!
I felt her!"

He just smiled.

"I know."

Step away

from the self-help section
of this rainy-day library

you won't find yourself there

instead
drown in poetry

and find that you
can finally breathe again

<u>I promise</u>

that one day
your sadness
will lose its comfort
and grow dull,

and you will
crave, instead,
the incredible
and innumerable
details
of daily life,
like

the dancing steam of tea,
the sounds and scents
of morning,
the blue
of the jay's wing,
and the mist
giving way
to the light

promising

the return of spring.

Spring Song

flowers grow
from my lungs
every time
I breathe
the sun in
at the dawn
hope will rise
from my eyes

the night will end

and this love
in my bones
roots deeper
in the dark

but I
am ready
to bloom

<u>To have roots,</u>

stay put,
cultivate a nest
of comfort and love.

Don't
run away.
Don't
mistake your roots
for chains.
You'll miss out
on essential nutrients.

To grow branches
and touch the sky,
create healthy change.
Tune to the seasons
of the land
and of your heart.

Don't
mistake bending
for breaking.
You'll miss out
on unexpected growth.

A tree stays put
yet is never
quite the same.

<u>I refuse</u>

to break.

I will bend
and bend
and bend

until the Universe
bends with me.

The First of June,
Methow Valley, WA

I am here,
and the fragrant silence
of the soft, lush mountains
pulses sweetly in my ears,
Broken only
by tree swallow song
and my own breath.

The trails are dotted
with mushrooms drying in the heat,
and grasses rustle with the retreat
of snakes and mice.

How can I express the relief
of simply Being,
undeterred by noise and crowds,
interrupted only by insects
landing, feather-light, on my skin?

Perhaps I should feel shame
for wishing to crawl beneath
the lupine and pine
and let the soil have its way with me --

certainly thoughts and concerns of my daughter
rest in the back and sides of my mind,
next to my goals and to-do lists.

But this moment,
the first of June,
is mine alone,
and I willingly share it
only with the birds
and the ants.

At the foot of the sacred mountain

she spoke a sermon of the trees
in the echoing cathedral of the valley,
where dew like strung stars glittered
on the dawn blanket of grass
and flowers breathed fragrance

waiting for the sun.

Vision Fast,
Methow Valley, WA, 2019

See me:
I am the sacred mountain.

My gentle, strong slopes
lush with pine and fir
beckon you
to be slow and peaceful
as the blue moth,
and sing as freely
as the birds making homes
in my eyes.

Crawl into my mouth.
Let me swallow you whole,
and digest you
in the pulsing heart of my night.

You do not need those old eyes;
take these instead:
the focus of the ant,
the cleverness of the coyote,
the silence of the deer,
the forethought of the bear,

the speed of the fly,
the sweet fierceness of the bee --

and your own honeyed tears,
dyed with the gold
of my slopes at dawn,
and the blush of wild rose
at dusk.

Lay in my stomach,
feed from me with the umbilical cord
of your sobs and prostrations,
your dirt kisses
and sky embraces.

I am destroying your once-was
with shooting stars
and phantom voices,
footsteps of spirit feet.

Let me dissolve your
maybe's and reluctant should's
like the rain dissolves
into my soil.

You have lent your soul to me,

left its prayers beneath quartz and smoke,
entrusted me with its care.

Let me rebuild your now-ness
with the woodpecker's violent carpentry
and the flower's gentle fragrance.

Do not fear me. Do not fear me.
See my vastness:
I am much larger than you think,
far darker than you can see.

Do not fear me. Do not fear me.
My meadow is the hand I extend,
and my foothills my breasts--
I invite you to suckle New Moon milk,
heavy with longing.

See me:
I am the sacred mountain.

Your body is my creation,
and though your feet now walk pavement
and fly in metallic imitation of my birds,
you feel the push and pull
of my womb's contractions.

You have not walked away from me,
I have birthed you
bloody and tender,
and you walk in an unsteady but certain dance
through inhumane streets
with feet growing moss and mushrooms.

Those feet will stumble,
that heart will flutter,
you will blink in confusion
and startle easily:
this is normal for the fawn.

I have birthed you whole
and you flowed down my legs with kisses and gasps,
not quite feeling the fullness of loss yet,

but there will be a time you will cry for your Mother,
hysterical hiccuping sobs muffled
into your pillow while your lover sleeps.

I will send you a letter,
the only one I can:
Look inside:
See me:

We
are the sacred mountain.

<u>a quiet way to become whole:</u>

discern
the trees.

stories
are woven
into the
placement

of their
branches
and
leaves.

Growth

does not happen
when we are in perfect balance.

Seek moments
of intensity

and follow them
with rest,

but do not forever seek
to be still
anywhere but within your soul.

A seed does not
become a flower

by remaining
in the silent comfort of its shell.

It must push against
its boundaries
with determination and passion.

Your form reflected

in the eternity of still pond water,
barely interrupted
by your wanderings.

This sunset light silhouetting you,
hiding your grin,
but not your joy.

I know I'll have to carry you home,
wrapped in an extra coat,
your legs soaked and shivering.

The other mothers keeping their kids
from going in, and I
can't help but let you

because I'm having visions of myself
in the Alaskan forest,
the consequences of the cold

worth pennies in comparison
to the priceless treasure
of wonder.

Co-parenting

We laughed
as we soaked in
memories,
driving beneath
a red evening sky,

red as the blood that
poured from me as I
birthed our child,

red as the unspoken
tinging the edges
of our guffaws,

knocking on the door
like shadows at the edge
of light,
tentative.

We left it behind
with the last echoes
of our giggles
vibrating into the night.

Tomorrow,
the dawn will come,
as it always does.

Some things I know for sure:

that the rain
is here to nurture us,
so I never sing
for it to go away.

That the sun
can blind us,
so when we're lost
we should look to the constellations.

That the land
speaks to us,
so if you're uncertain,
lay down on the forest floor.

That silence
is as important as sound,
so we must eat stillness
as often as we drink music.

That aloneness
is not the same as loneliness,
so we should learn to be solitary
and love it as we love good company.

<u>sacred alone</u>

Candle light,
morning mist and rain,
the lush green.
Piano, quiet,
peaceful pervading
space of few words.

My mind and heart
may feel heavy,
but this moment is light,
just steam rising
in gentle waltzes
off hot coffee.

Day: let me carry
the gentleness of this
soft dawn
into the busy hours
of city life.

Now, breath.
Aloneness.
Room to Be.

The birds sing
and cars roar
between wild trees.

<u>October, 2019</u>

Like a tree,
I return to my roots

loving again the comfort
of soil
and letting my bare branches

dance in the cold breeze,
while I commune with
the magic of fungus and moss

and the dark truths
of Being.

This:

the dawn
not breaking
the night,
but rather,
the night
birthing
the dawn,

painting
the colors of day
with brushstrokes
of borrowed starlight
and the trill
of morning birds:

peace rising
from restless
heartache,

shadows
forming
light,

sacred laughter

rising from
the sleepless throes

of black midnight.

re-Connection

We Remember ourselves
through our connections,

like these windswept dunes in sunlight
joyful crashing waves
dripping rainbow moss sunset

and these people
made of dreams
stitched together with hope
illuminated by surrender.

I Remember myself
where walls dissolve.

Soak me in tenderness.
Dance me with love.
Together, we Remember ourselves.

www.ingramcontent.com/pod-product-compliance
Lightning Source LLC
Chambersburg PA
CBHW032208040426
42449CB00005B/488